A Lucky Thing

POEMS BY

ALICE SCHERTLE

PAINTINGS BY

WENDELL MINOR

Browndeer Press

Harcourt Brace & Company

SAN DIEGO   NEW YORK   LONDON

Browndeer Press is a registered trademark of Harcourt Brace & Company.

Library of Congress Cataloging-in-Publication Data
Schertle, Alice.
A lucky thing/poems by Alice Schertle; paintings by Wendell Minor.
p. cm.
"Browndeer Press."
Summary: A collection of fourteen poems about nature, including
"Calling the Sun," "Showing the Wind," and "Invitation from a Mole."
ISBN 0-15-200541-2
1. Children's poetry, American. 2. Nature—Juvenile poetry.
[1. Nature—Poetry. 2. American poetry.]
I. Minor, Wendell, ill. II. Title.
PS3569.C48435L83 1999
811'.54—dc21 97-43166

First edition
A C E F D B

PRINTED IN HONG KONG

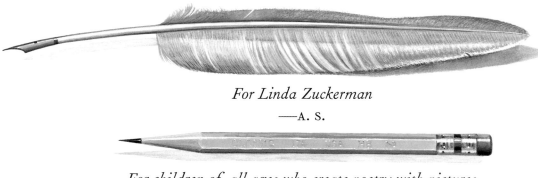

For Linda Zuckerman

—A. S.

For children of all ages who create poetry with pictures

—W. M.

Right Here

Right here
on this
        clean
white page

I'll scatter some words,
        watch them grow.
        I'll plant
a meadow.

I'll dig a pond right here.
Dig down deep until
        the water
        and the words
        run clear.

I'll build me a barn.
        Lay the lines out straight and
raise the roof!

        Write
here.

THE BARN

All night
its creaking timbers
rode the storm,
the old blunt prow
lifting bravely
above dark waves
of rain.

Now
the sagging roof steams
in the first rays
of sun.
Battered doors askew,
it lies beached,
dripping,
on a low rise
behind the henhouse.

From the damp shadows
of its hold,
the stamping, snorting
voyagers come forward
two by two.

SHOWING THE WIND

On top of the barn,
against the sky,
a flat black bird with a hollow eye,
metal wings and an iron beak,
clings to an arrow. A rusty squeak
is the rooster's crow.
He points the way
for the wind to go.

North   East   West   South

squeak ...
            he turns with an open mouth

squeak ...
            he turns with a rusty wail
            crowing the way
            to gust or gale

North   South   East   West

            showing the wind
            which way is best
            to blow.

Calling the Sun

He stands
on a post
where the greens will show,
and the reds and golds
and the blues. They glow
when he calls up the sun
       (if the weather's fine)
and it falls on his feathers
and the colors
shine.

He wakes the world so the world
will know
how the sun
comes running
when a loud proud crow
says a rooster's ready and the sun
       may rise
and gaze at itself
in a rooster's eyes.

A Lucky Thing

High
up in a hawthorn tree
a robin perched, where he could see
into a coop of wire and wood.
Inside the coop a farmer stood
flinging grain upon the ground.
Twelve fat chickens gathered round.

The robin,
singing, cocked his head
and watched the chickens being fed.
He saw it was a lucky thing
to be a chicken: Farmers bring
you golden grain, scoop after scoop,
if you're a chicken in a coop—
a lovely coop with nesting boxes
safe from cats and crows and foxes.

The chickens
in the coop could see
the bird. They heard his melody
and clucked it was a lucky thing
to be a robin who could sing
a song upon a hawthorn tree.
They watched him through the woven
wire.
They saw him fly up high, and higher.

Twelve fat chickens
scratched the floor.
The farmer closed
and latched
the door.

SCARECROW

Last night, alone, he saw the rising moon
set silver fires among his stalks of corn
and watched the tassels burn like candlewicks.
At dawn he saw the noisy crows return.
They know him for a friend, this man of sticks
in boots that dangle just above the dirt,
the handle of a rake shoved through his shirt.

On summer days when grass around him sways
like wave that follows wave upon the ocean,
I've seen him shake, a dancer on a stake,
as if he feels a music in the motion.
And once I saw his round astonished eyes
observe with more than painted-on surprise
a black snake flow like water down a hole,
and heard him sigh upon his wooden pole.

POEM ABOUT RABBIT

I am writing a poem
     about

     rabbit.

A pink-eyed poem
     that watches
          from the
edges
of the page,
     that nibbles
          at the
corners
of my mind.

     A quiet poem.

The kind
          with long-eared lines that   listen
to where the words fall.

A poem
coming close
     enough to touch,

standing

    still

to watch
me write a poem
    about

       rabbit.

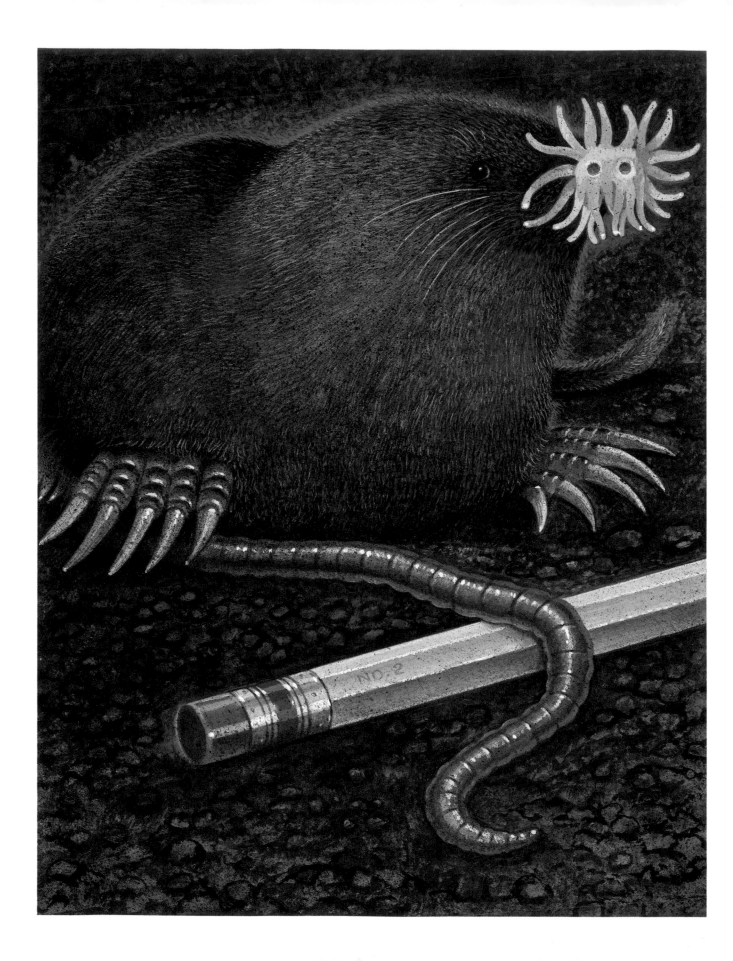

Invitation from a Mole

come on down

live among worms awhile
taste dirt
　　　on the tip of your tongue

smell
　　　the sweet damp feet of mushrooms
listen to roots
　　　　　reaching
　　　　　　　　deeper
press your cheek against
the cold face of a stone

wear the earth like a glove
close   your   eyes
wrap yourself in darkness

　　　see

what you're missing

FROM A DISTANCE...

They look

like the
soft gray caps of mushrooms
too big to be believed.

Sandbags.

Burlap sacks of   something.

Sometimes they look just
like piles of laundry.

Plumped-up pillows.

Lumps of clay.

They look like old tombstones
sunk down shoulder deep.

Then one starts moving off
across the meadow
and all
the others   follow,
just

like sheep.

HEAD FULL OF TURTLE

Stuck   in a skull shell

under
            a bone
dome

there's a turtle in my head

Got to get rid
of the cold smell
of mud   on my mind

Got to find
a way to nudge this old slow stepper across the   page

get him to put
            one
                  stump
of a foot   in the book

Move it, Mud Lump
take a chance   budge a bit

Do it, Old Stout

just once

stick

your

neck

out

POND

Their delicate mouths dripping,
deer raise
their heads
from the pond

to watch
the cows
wading out
among water lilies.

ONE

From one gray cloud
came a single drop
and it fell
in the pond
with one wet

Plop!

"Deep! Deep! Deep!"
sang one small peeper
when he saw
that the pond
was one drop

deeper.

From one g
came a sin
and it
in a
wit

A Traditional Frog's Curse

May you live
      among cranes.

May you wait for rains
      that never come.

May every stream
      that fills your pond
      run dry

and every fly
      stay just beyond
      your tongue.

WRITING PAST MIDNIGHT

insects drone ... the night draws on ...
I am writing a poem about a barn ...

and my room is warm with the breath of horses
and dust from the loft runs in streams down the walls
and somewhere the sound
                              of sheep snoring softly
blends with the hum of computers
                              asleep in their stalls

bundled with bailing wire
                              stanzas
                              are stacked
                              to the ceiling

spiderwebs anchor the edge of my desk to the floor
a small gray verse runs squeaking down one of the rafters

just as the moon floats in through the double barn door

The illustrations in this book were
done in watercolor on illustration board.
The display type was set in Mazurka.
The text type was set in Fournier.
Color separations by Bright Arts Ltd., Hong Kong
Printed by South China Printing Company, Ltd., Hong Kong
This book was printed on totally chlorine-free Nymolla Matte Art paper.
Production supervision by Stanley Redfern and Ginger Boyer
Designed by Michael Farmer